GRANDTULLY
PRIMARY SCHOOL

# STEP-by-STEP

## SCIENCE

# Colour

## Robert Snedden and Sabrina Crewe

### Illustrated by Stuart Lafford, Raymond Turvey and Joanna Williams

# FRANKLIN WATTS

## LONDON • SYDNEY

D0347703

© Franklin Watts 1998
This edition 2002

First Published in Great Britain by Franklin Watts
96 Leonard Street London EC2A 4XD

Franklin Watts Australia
56 O'Riordan Street
Alexandria, Sydney
NSW 2015

ISBN 0 7496 4577 6 (pbk)

Dewey Decimal Classification 535.6

A CIP catalogue record for this book is available from the British Library

Printed in Dubai

Planning and production by Discovery Books Ltd
Design: Ian Winton
Editor: Helena Attlee
Consultant: Jeremy Bloomfield


Photographs: Bridgeman Art Library/Musee de l'Orangerie, Paris/Lauros-Giraudon
(Claude Monet **Argenteuil** 1872-5); Bruce Coleman: page 5 right (Kevin Burchett), 19 top (Michael
McCoy), 21 (Andy Purcell), 22 top (Jane Burton), 22 bottom (Konrad Wothe), 23 top (Joe McDonald),
23 bottom (C C Lockwood); Getty Images: page 6 (Andy Sacks), 17 top (Lori Adamski Peek), 18
(Bruce Forster), 26 (Gary Yeowell), 29 (Michael Scott); Robert Harding Picture Library: page 11, 14, 17
bottom, 24; The Image Bank: page 4 (Terje Rakke), 5 (left) (Jeff Hunter), 7 (Weinberg/Clark), 12
(right), 19 (Bottom) (Grant V Faint), 29 bottom (Don Landwehrle); Oxford Scientific Films:
page 31 bottom (Alastair Shay); Redferns Music Picture Library: page 31 top (S Morley);
Science Photo Library: page 25 both (C Nuridsany/M Perennou);
Spectrum Colour Library: page 12 left, ZEFA: cover.

# Contents

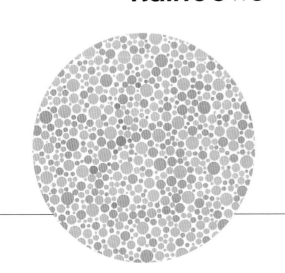

# A Colourful World

Imagine a world without colour. These colourful sailing-boats would seem quite different...

...if they were in black and white.

We use colour all the time to describe things, and to tell them apart. We use colours to paint imaginary worlds of our own. The colours of nature make the real world a beautiful place.

We are lucky to live in a very colourful world. Bright colours make us feel happy. We can use colours to cheer ourselves up on a grey day.

# Primary Colours

When you paint a picture, you may want to use many colours. You can make hundreds of colours by mixing different paints together.

There are three colours you need to make all other colours. Red, yellow and blue are called **primary colours**. Primary colours can't be made by mixing other colours. But if you have red, yellow and blue, you can mix all the colours you want!

# Mixing Colours

What happens when you mix blue with yellow? You make green. Green isn't a primary colour, so you have to mix other colours to make it. Mixing yellow with red makes orange. Mixing red with blue makes purple. What happens if you mix many colours together?

YELLOW

GREEN

Artists mix little dabs of colour together on a palette until they get just the colour they want.

# Shades of Colour

When you make a paint paler or darker, you are changing its **shade**. To make colours paler, you must add white. Blue becomes pale blue. Red becomes pink. If you want to change a colour to a darker shade, you can add black.

| Red | Pink | White |
|-----|------|-------|

## MAKING SHADES

You can make a shade chart by choosing a colour and making it darker and lighter. You will need poster paints in black, white and one other colour, such as a bright blue.

**1** Put two blobs of blue paint on a plate. Now paint a stripe down the middle of a piece of paper.

**2** Add a few drops of white to your blue paint and mix it in. Paint a paler stripe to the left of your first one. Continue to paint paler and paler stripes by adding more white paint.

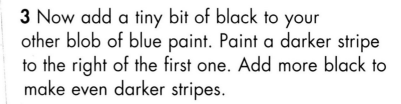

**3** Now add a tiny bit of black to your other blob of blue paint. Paint a darker stripe to the right of the first one. Add more black to make even darker stripes.

Painters use light and dark shades of many colours in one painting. When you look from far away, you may see the colours all blended together. When you look up close, you can see tiny brushstrokes in different shades and colours.

# Pigments

The tiny pieces of colour that are used to make paints are called **pigments**. Many pigments come from plants and animals. Others come from rocks. Long ago, these natural pigments were the only colours that people had.

Natural pigments usually make soft, rich colours. Many of the bright colours we have today are not natural. They are made from **chemicals**.

Thousands of years ago, the first artists used natural pigments to paint animals on the walls of caves. The cave painters made their paint by grinding up coloured rocks and charcoal. They used twigs, leaves and blowpipes to paint the mixture on the walls.

## Sistine Chapel

This is the Sistine Chapel in Italy. The chapel was painted hundreds of years ago. The artists used paints made from natural pigments.

# Making Dyes

Dyes are used to colour things when the colour needs to last. People use dyes for colouring clothes, paper and food.

All paints used to be made from plant juices, shellfish, insects and other natural materials.

Today, most dyes are made with chemicals. Chemical dyes make many bright colours for clothes and other things.

# VEGETABLE COLOURS

You can make your own vegetable dyes and use them to dye a piece of white fabric, such as an old T-shirt or handkerchief. You can use onion skins, which will give you a yellow dye, or beetroot, which will give you a pink dye.

**1** Ask an adult to boil some onion skins or beetroot with a little water in an old saucepan. The mixture should simmer for about fifteen minutes.

**2** Leave the mixture to cool. Ask your adult helper to pour the coloured liquid through a strainer into a bowl.

**3** Take a piece of fabric and put it into the bowl. Make sure all the fabric gets soaked in the dye.

**4** After the fabric has soaked for a few minutes, take it out of the bowl and squeeze it out. Then hang it up to dry.

# Colour Power

How do colours make you feel? What do they make you think of? A brightly coloured room will create a different mood from a room painted in pale, cool colours.

## Moody Colours

Green makes us think of leaves and trees in cool, shady places. It can make people feel relaxed.

Blue is a cold colour. It makes us think of water and ice.

Some colours grab your attention. When yellow and black are used together, they are very easy to see. That's why these colours are often used on roads. It is very important that drivers notice them.

Red is also easy to see. Many warning signs are coloured red to help people spot them. If a red flag is flying on the beach, people can see from a distance that it is not safe to swim.

Red is the colour of hot things, and makes us think of danger and excitement.

Yellow is a sunny colour, and makes us feel warm.

# Colourful Messages

Z

Colours are very useful for sending signals. Messages using coloured lights or flags can be understood all over the world. In many countries, traffic lights flash red for 'stop' and green for 'go'.

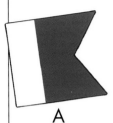

A

B

C

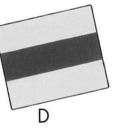

D

E

Coloured lights are used by aeroplanes at night. Aeroplanes have red lights on the left wing, green lights on the right wing, and white lights on their tail. This shows pilots where other aeroplanes are and which way they are going.

F

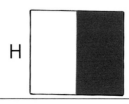

G

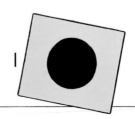

H

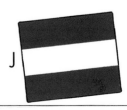

I

J

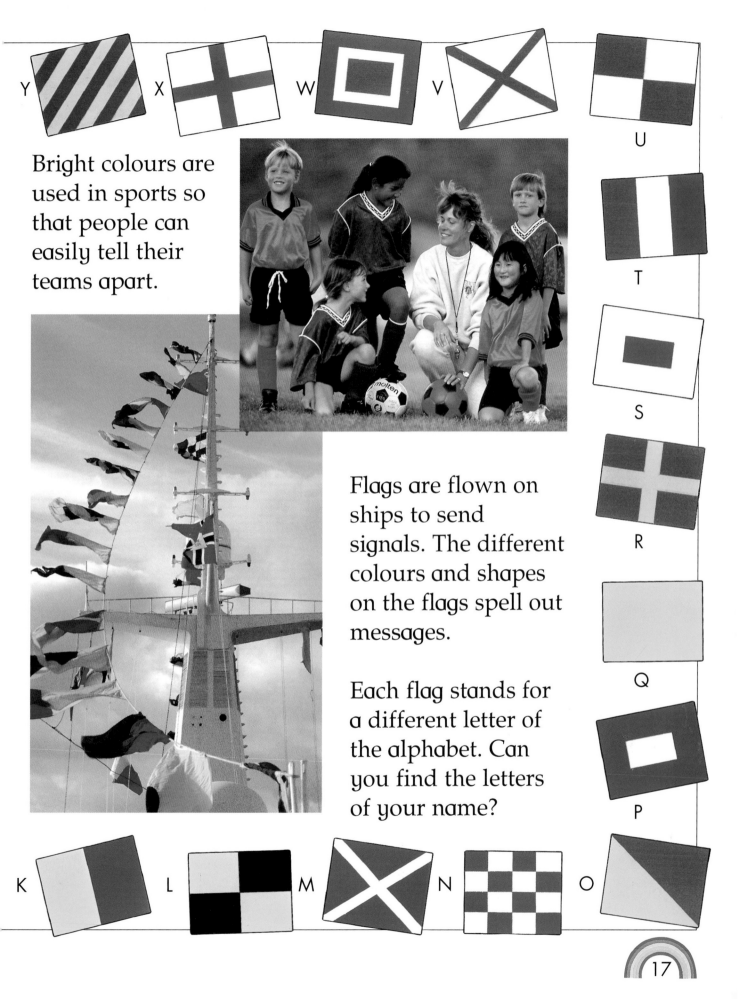

Y    X    W    V    U
T
S
R
Q
P

Bright colours are used in sports so that people can easily tell their teams apart.

Flags are flown on ships to send signals. The different colours and shapes on the flags spell out messages.

Each flag stands for a different letter of the alphabet. Can you find the letters of your name?

K    L    M    N    O

# People Colours

Blue

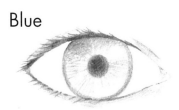

Have you ever wondered why people have different skin, hair and eye colour? It has to do with different amounts of pigment. Skin, hair and eyes get their colours from pigment in our bodies.

Green

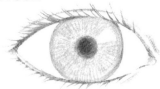

Everybody's skin is the same, except that pale skin has less pigment in it than dark skin. Different amounts of pigment can make all hair colours, from pale blonde and red to black.

Brown

People have always used colours to decorate their skin and dye their hair.

This man from Papua New Guinea has painted his face in a traditional way.

Sometimes people paint their faces just for fun.

# Animal Colours

Many animals are brightly coloured. Sometimes their colours warn other animals that they are poisonous or can sting.

Some birds are very brightly coloured. Male birds are usually brighter than females. Males sit where they can easily be seen, showing their coloured feathers. They do this to protect their **territory**. Male birds also **attract** female birds with their bright colours.

Some animals use bright colours to confuse their **predators**. If a hungry bird approaches the red underwing moth, it shows its red and black underwings to frighten the bird away.

# Camouflage

Some animals are hard to see. The colours and patterns of their fur or skin are like the colours of their surroundings. This is called **camouflage**. Camouflage helps to protect many animals from predators.

Chameleons can change their colour to match their background.

The stripes of a tiger look striking out in the open. But the tiger blends well with the light and shade in long grass. This helps the tiger to hunt other animals.

People sometimes use camouflage, too. Soldiers camouflage themselves to hide from enemies.

This mountain hare is brown in summer, but in winter it grows a new white coat to help it hide against the snow.

# Flower Colours

Flowers come in many bright colours. These colours attract insects, who go to flowers to collect nectar and pollen. When they do this, they help the flowers to make seeds.

Some flowers have special pigments which people can't see. These pigments make colours which are only seen in **ultraviolet** light. Bees and other insects use ultraviolet light to see and so they can see the colours that are invisible to us.

### Bee's Eye View

The photograph on the left shows how a potentilla flower looks to us.

The special photograph on the right shows us what it would look like to a bee. The dark patches on the petals show bees and other insects the way to the flower's nectar.

Plants that are visited by moths often have white flowers. Moths look for their food at night and white shows up in the dark better than other colours.

# Rainbows

Have you ever seen a rainbow in the sky when it is raining? Where do you think the colours come from?

Sunlight looks white but it contains light of many colours. When it rains, sunlight hits the raindrops. The light bends and splits into separate bands of colour. These are the colours you see when you look at a rainbow.

The colours you see in a rainbow are called the colours of the **spectrum**. When raindrops bend sunlight, some of the colours bend more than others. Red bends most and violet bends least. That's why we see them as separate bands.

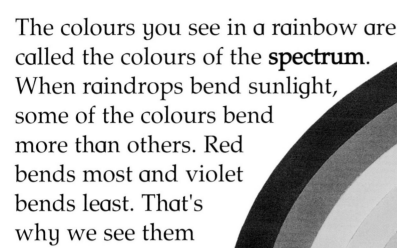

Red

Orange

Yellow

Green

Blue

Violet

## MAKE A RAINBOW SPINNER

You can mix the colours of the spectrum back together to make white.

**1** Cut out a circle about 15 cm across from a piece of white cardboard.

**2** Make a rainbow disc by colouring your circle with the colours of the spectrum. Use coloured pencils so that your colours are pale.

**3** Ask an adult to make a hole in the middle of the card. Push a pencil through the hole to make a spinning disc.

**4** Spin the rainbow disc as fast as you can. What happens to the colours?

# Seeing Colours

Sunlight contains light of many colours. When sunlight shines on an object, some colours in the light are **absorbed** and others are reflected. The reflected light bounces off the object and into our eyes. The colour of the reflected light is the colour that we see.

### Animal Vision

Many animals see the world with very little colour. They see mostly in black, white and grey.

A strawberry reflects red light, and so we see it as red. The leaves of a plant reflect green light and so we would see them as green. The colour reflected by different things depends on what they are made of.

## Colour Blindness

People who are colour blind have trouble seeing colours. They may not be able to tell red from green. Look at this pattern of coloured spots. Can you see a number in the pattern? A colour blind person could not see it because the colours would all look the same.

The parts of our eyes that pick up colours don't work in the dark. If there is a little bit of light we can still see shapes and objects, but not their colours.

# Colour Filters

If you look through a coloured piece of cellophane, the colours you see will seem strange. A coloured sheet of plastic, glass or cellophane only lets through light that is the same colour as itself. It is acting as a **filter**.

A green filter will only let through green light. If you look at a red object through a green filter, it will appear black.

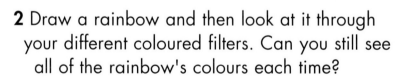

## FILTER FUN

You can have fun making your own coloured filters.

**1** Find some coloured cellophane or plastic, such as sweet wrappers or plastic folders.

**2** Draw a rainbow and then look at it through your different coloured filters. Can you still see all of the rainbow's colours each time?

**3** Look at other things through your filters and see if they change colour.

**4** Put your filters over a torch to make different coloured lights. Shine your torch on the wall and see how the filters change the colour of the light.

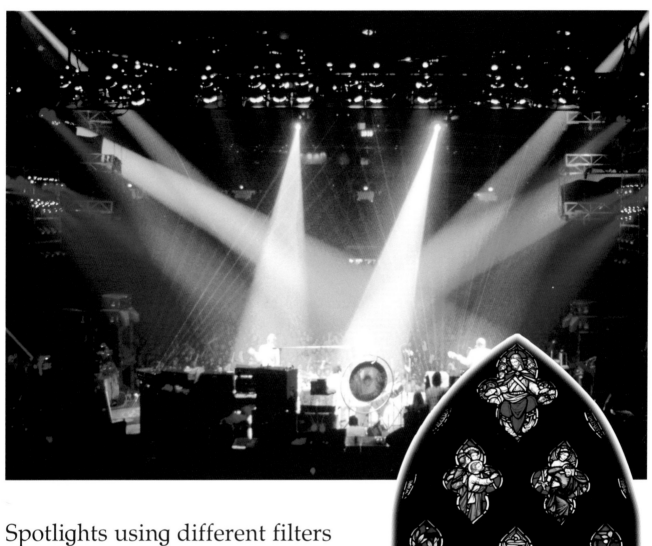

Spotlights using different filters
can make wonderful colours
appear on a stage.

The sunlight comes into this
church through a stained glass
window. Each piece of different
coloured glass only lets through
light of its own colour.

# Glossary

**Absorbed:** When the colours in light are taken in by an object instead of being reflected we say that they have been absorbed

**Attract:** To get the attention of another person or animal

**Camouflage:** Colours or markings that blend in with the background and help to hide animals or objects

**Chemicals:** The many substances that mix together in different ways to make all living and non-living things

**Filter:** Something that only lets through some of the colours in light. The colours that pass through depend on the colour of the filter itself

**Pigments:** Coloured substances that give colour to other things

**Predators:** Animals that hunt and kill other animals for food

**Primary colours:** Colours that cannot be made by mixing other colours, but can be used to make other colours

**Shade:** Darker and lighter versions of the same colour

**Spectrum:** The spread of colours that can be seen when white light is split up.

**Territory:** The area that an animal defends as its own

**Ultraviolet:** A part of the light spectrum that comes after violet and can't be seen by people

# Index